Daisy- Innocence, purity
Origin- Europe, Western Asia

Dandelion—Faithfulness
Origin- Native to Eurasia

Cleome—Elope with me
Origin- Native to South America

Coreopsis—Always cheerful
Origin- native to North and
South America

Gardenia—You're lovely
Origin- Africa, Asia, Madagascar

Iris - Your friendship means a lot
Origin- Europe, Asia, and North America

Lily-Walking on air
Origin- Europe, Asia, North America

Mistletoe—Affection
Origin- Europe, Asia, North America

Bluebell—Humility

Origin- Western Europe

Myrtle—Love
Origin- Mediterranean region

Nasturtium - victory in battle
Origin- South and Central America

Orchid—Love, beauty
Origin- Tropical regions

Rosebud—Beauty and you
Origin- Worldwide

Azalea—Take care of yourself
Origin- North America and Europe.

Tiger lily—Wealth

Origin- China, Japan,Korea

Smilax—Loveliness

Origin- tropical and temperate regions

Moss—Maternal love

Origin- Worldwide

Calla—Beauty
Origin- Southern Africa

Amaryllis—Pride
Origin- South Africa, South America

Violet—Modesty

Origin- Europe, Asia

Hibiscus—Delicate beauty

Origin- Tropical and subtropical regions

Zinnia mixed—Thoughts of friends
Origin- United States, South America

Hyacinth—Sincerity

Origin- Eastern Mediterranean

Fern—Magic
Origin- Worldwide

Chrysanthemum red - Deep passion
Origin- Asia, Northeastern Europe

Forsythia- New beginnings
Origin- Asia and southeastern Europe

Cactus—Endurance

Origin- Americas

Bells-of-Ireland—Good luck
Origin- Western Asia, Mediterranean

Aster—Symbol of love
Origin- Europe, Asia, North America

Lily-of-the-valley- Return of happiness
Origin- Europe, Asia

Alstroemeria - Friendship
Origin- South America

Anemone - Protection
Origin- Europe, North America, Asia

Apple Blossom - Good fortune
Origin- Asia, Europe, North America

Begonia - Deep thinking
Origin- America, Africa, Asia

Camellia - Gratitude
Origin- Southeast Asia

Bourvardia - Enthusiasm
Origin- Central and South America

Cheery Blossom - Transient nature of life

Origin- Asia

Carnation - Fascination

Origin- Mediterranean region

Crocus - Youthful gladness

Origin- Europe, Asia, and North Africa

Corn Poppy - Consolation
Origin- Europe, Asia, North Africa

Cypress- Sorrow
Origin- Northern Hemisphere

Daffodil - New beginnings
Origin- Europe and North Africa

Forget-Me-Nots - Memories
Origin- Europe and Asia

Dahlia - Elegance and dignity
Origin- Mexico

Gerbera - Innocence and purity
Origin- South America, Africa, and Asia

Freesia - Trust
Origin- South Africa

Gladiolus - Strength of character
Origin- Africa, Mediterranean Europe

Heather - Admiration and good luck
Origin- Europe and Asia

Laurel - Glory and honor
Origin- Mediterranean region

Hydrangea - Heartfelt emotions
Origin- Asia and the Americas

Lilac - First love
Origin- Europe and Asia

Lavender - Devotion and love
Origin- Mediterranean, India, Middle East

Lisianthus - Appreciation

Origin- Southern United States to Mexico

Lotus- Purity
Origin-Asia, Australia,North America

Marigold - Sacred affection
Origin-Mexico, Central America

Magnolia - Love for nature
Origin- Americas, Southeast Asia

Orchids - Rare Beauty
Origin- Worldwide tropical regions

Morning Glory - Affection
Origin- Central and South America

Proteas - Diversity and courage
Origin- South Africa and Australia

Peace Lily - Peace and rebirth
Origin- Asia and the Americas

Snapdragon - Graciousness

Origin- Europe and North America

Ranunculus- Radiant charm
Origin- Asia and Europe

Stock - You'll always be beautiful to me
Origin- Southern Europe, Western Asia

Statice - Remembrance
Origin- Southern Europe, Western Asia

Sweet Pea - Pleasure

Origin- Sicily and southern Italy

Sunflower - Adoration and loyalty
Origin- Americas

Tulips - Declaration of love
Origin- Central Asia and Turkey

Water Lily - Purity and majesty
Origin- Worldwide

Umbrella Plant - Protection
Origin- Asia and Australia

Rosemary - Remembrance
Origin- Mediterranean region

Pansy - Thoughtfulness

Origin- Europe and western Asia

Quince Blossom - Temptation
Origin- Southwest Asia

Mimosa - Sensitivity

Origin- Australia

Oleander - Caution
Origin- Mediterranean region, Asia

Impatiens - Motherly love
Origin- Northern Hemisphere

Kangaroo Paw - Diversity
Origin- Australia

Hellebore - Scandal
Origin- Europe and Asia

Globe Thistle - Unchanging love
Origin- Europe and Asia

Euphorbia - Persistence

Origin- Worldwide

Foxglove - Insincerity
Origin- Europe, western, Asia

Bellflower - Gratitude

Origin- Northern Hemisphere

Yarrow - Healing
Origin- Northern Hemisphere

Wisteria - Welcome

Origin-United States, China, Japan

Xeranthemum - Eternity
Origin- Southern Europe

Bearberry - Think of me
Origin- Northern Hemisphere

Sea Lavender - Remembrance
Origin- Eurasia

Queen Anne's Lace - Sanctuary
Origin - Europe and Asia

Primrose - Young love
Origin- Europe and Asia

Nigella - Perseverance
Origin- Europe to Asia

Oxeye Daisy- Patience
Origin- Europe, Western Asia

Lantana- Rigor

Origin- Americas , Africa

Monkshood - Deadly foe is near
Origin- Northern Hemisphere

Jacob's Ladder - Come down
Origin- North America, Europe

Kalmia - Treachery
Origin- North America

Heliotrope - Eternal love
Origin- Peru

Gladiolus—Strength of character
Origin- Africa , Mediterranean Europe

Edelweiss -Purity, courage
Origin- European Alps

Bleeding Heart - Undying love
Origin- Asia , North America

Aconitum —Caution

Origin- Greek

Bulbous Buttercup - Attractiveness
Origin- Europe, Asia, North Africa